The Mental Toughness Workbook:

A 6-Week Resilience Training Program

Peter Graham

If you enjoy reading this book then please consider leaving a review. Scan the U.S or U.K QR code below to be taken directly to the review page.

U.S

U.K

<u>Special Bonus!</u>

Want this Bonus Book for
FREE?

Get FREE, unlimited access to it
and all of my new books by
joining my Fan Base!

SCAN
W/YOUR
CAMERA
TO JOIN!

Table of Contents

How to use this workbook

This workbook is to be used in conjunction with the book "The Power of Mental Toughness: A Practical Guide To Improving Your Self-Discipline, Gain Self-Confidence And Build Mental Resilience For Success."

Mental toughness is something that *can* be cultivated. With the help of this personal workbook, it is possible to develop the right mentality needed to become mentally robust, regardless of your starting point. I only ask that the reader complete all exercises and instructions in this book to the best of their abilities.

In Part 1 of this workbook, we will be exploring what mental toughness is. What your current level of mental toughness is and the principles and values that are needed to achieve your goals and ambitions.

In Part 2 I'll show you how to achieve your goals and ambitions.

Are you ready?

1.

PART 1. WHAT IS MENTAL TOUGHNESS?

"It is not the mountain we conquer, but ourselves."
– Sir Edmund Hillary

Perhaps one of the most important factors to success in life is mental toughness. The ability to keep going when the going gets tough is something that separates the extraordinary person from the ordinary. What makes some people great is the fact that they persevere when others give up. They believe that where there's a will, there's a way. No matter how many times they fall down, they never fail to get up. They have no time to feel sorry for themselves or blame others for their challenges. They see each challenge as a hurdle they have to jump in order to achieve the next level of greatness.

The difference between champions and everyone else is that champions don't do what's needed only when they feel like it. I want to emphasize here that mental toughness is built with habits, not through motivation. You can't wait for motivation to strike or you would spend your entire life being a bystander.

To be mentally tough, you have to study the habits of successful people and incorporate those habits into your own life. Once you commit yourself to those habits, you don't give yourself any room for an exit. You do what's needed every single day whether you are feeling like it or not. Average people are too focused on their feelings. They allow themselves to be ruled by their emotions. They'll do something when they are 'feeling like it' or they won't do something because they aren't 'feeling like it.'

If you want to achieve an elite level of mental toughness then you do what's needed, not when it's easy or convenient, but when it needs to be done.

Understanding *your* current level of Mental Toughness

Measuring somebody's physical strength or cardiovascular abilities is a rather easy task but trying to understand your current level of mental toughness isn't an easy thing to do. After all, how do you measure something that isn't physical? What this requires is a person to really think and reflect deeply about themselves and the choices they've made so far in life. This is far from easy as sometimes we can be too hard on ourselves and at other times, we let ourselves get away with things we otherwise wouldn't allow.

You may well be mentally tough in certain aspects of your life, such as your job and in other areas you may not be, such as your fitness. Most people are OK with this but what separates OK people and GREAT – ordinary and extraordinary people is the ability to have control over all aspects of your life. Mentally tough people are constantly focused on solutions. They know that there's a way out of everything. Finding the way and emerging victorious at the other end of every dark tunnel is what builds character. What makes one person a champion and another one an average is their ability to tolerate pain. The average person lives with the pain of regrets, constantly making excuses for why they can't have what they desire.

Below is a questionnaire that will help gauge your current level of mental toughness. Try to be honest with yourself but don't be too harsh either. Reflection is important so take some time completing this if needed.

Scores from 1-10. 1 meaning not at all and 10 meaning absolutely.	1-10
1. I believe that I can achieve anything I set my mind to.	
2. I believe I have full control over all aspects of my life.	
3. I have the confidence in my abilities to achieve my desired goals and ambitions.	
4. I have the confidence in my abilities to try new things I'm interested in.	
5. I have a solid record of completing my goals and objectives.	
6. My environment is free from distractions and enables me to perform at my best.	
7. I generally look after my health, including my physical fitness, my mental wellbeing and my emotions.	
8. I actively look for ways to improve all aspects of my life.	
9. My goals align with my core values.	
10. The goals and dreams I am actively pursuing are mine and mine alone.	
TOTAL SCORE	

0-30 Just Getting Started

30-60 Well On My Way

60-75 Amateur Mental Toughness

75-90 Pro Mental Toughness

90-100 Elite Mental Toughness

The Mental Toughness Workbook

Principles and values of mentally tough people

Mentally tough people all have principles and values that they hold close to their hearts and are willing to fight and die for. These values are the very essence of what makes them who they are. We all have values in our lives, even when we do not think that we do. Choosing the easy option all the time is a value, it's the path of least resistance. The path to mediocrity. Mentally tough people live their lives with values and principles that better them as humans, that enable them to attain true peak performance in their field and benefit not just themselves but the communities they surround themselves in.

Some people may swear by certain values and principles and others not so much. Some people may value traditions whilst others are more open to change. Just like your *why* you have to believe in your values and principles too. Below are some of the values that I believe in.

- Integrity: Integrity is not just about telling the truth. It's about how you maintain your values and principles even when no one is looking.
- Self-Discipline: Resist the easy option. Much like integrity Self-Discipline is easy to resist when isolated. It's about doing what you have to do when you have to do it. Every single time.
- Humility: Respect the rights, diversity, and contribution of others.
- Excellence: Strive to do better. Always perform to the best of your abilities and strive to reach higher levels of achievement.

My question to *you* is, what are your core values and principles?

List up to 3 current values and principles you believe you have, good or bad:

1.
2.
3.

Now list up to 3 principles you wish to have. These can all be the same, some of them be the same or something new entirely:

1.

2.

3.

What would you do if you had the desired Mental Toughness?

If you had all the mental toughness in the world, what would you do with it? Do you think you would have a different job or be somewhere else in your life? What type of person do you think you would be? Would you be happier, driven, and content? By sitting down and thinking about these things you can better understand your thought process and come to a conclusion about why you want what you want. This is an important first step. Often we throw ourselves head first into new adventures, new goals and dreams but how often do we ask ourselves if it's what we really want? After all, if you're trying something out for the sake of it because it's trendy or because your friend said you should do it, how well do you think you will actually do it? This is why *your why* is so important.

Mental toughness won't offer solutions to all your problems immediately but it will arm you with a toolbox for better dealing with your feelings, emotions and events throughout your life.

Write down what you would do if you had the desired mental toughness. For example, you are stuck in a job you do not like. How would having mental toughness help change this? Or, you feel that your fitness and eating habits need an upgrade. How can having mental toughness help you achieve your goals?

_____

_____

_____

_____

_____

Your Why

Understanding *your why* is critical. It'll get you out of bed in the morning when the rest of the world is sleeping. It'll push you to keep on fighting when seemingly all the odds are stacked against you. It'll get you to put one front in front of the other, time and time again. But it has to be *your* why.

It's easy to desire many things in life simultaneously but for the purpose of this book I would like you to focus on one thing, one goal. The reason for this is simple. Not only can it be unproductive it can be extremely overwhelming trying to tackle several things at once, especially when new or difficult.

Inherently, most goals, dreams or ambitions will require multiple 'small' tasks. An example could be completing a marathon. This would entail an efficient running program, a detailed nutritious diet and perhaps research into running equipment that will aid you such as a running watch, shoes etc.

With that said I would like you to write down the one goal you desire to achieve. This could be personally or professionally. Try not to write just the goal, such as 'complete marathon' but write *why* you want it. Write how it would make you feel to achieve it and how it would make you feel if you didn't try. Write down if you think it will change you and in which ways. Fill in the blanks below:

Desired goal/ambition:

_____

_____

_____

Why do I want this?

The Mental Toughness Workbook

_____

_____

_____

How would it make me feel to achieve my goal?

_____

_____

_____

How would it make me feel if I never achieved this?

_____

_____

_____

How do I think this will change me for the good? List up to 5 things. For example, completing X will give me the confidence to try Y.

1.

2.

3.

4.

5.

The Mental Toughness Workbook

What will stop me from doing this? List up to 5 things. For example, my fear of failure.

1.

2.

3.

4.

5.

What do I need to do to achieve this? List up to 5 things. For example, create efficient daily habits.

1.

2.

3.

4.

5.

2

PART 2. YOUR ROADMAP TO MENTAL TOUGHNESS

Ask 'what is so unbearable about this situation? Why can't you endure it?' You will be embarrassed to answer.
– Marcus Aurelius

Mental toughness is not just about achieving a goal in itself. Mental toughness is the accumulation of events that happen in your life and how you let them define you. It's overcoming adversity, disappointment and expectations. Mentally tough people get up when they get knocked down.

Every single time.

In the first part of this workbook, we measured your current level of mental toughness and what your focus of this book will be (your goal). This part of the book now serves as your roadmap to achieving that goal.

Complete all the exercises and instructions with integrity and self-regard.

Week 1

Create a winning environment

"If not now, when?"
– Hillel the Elder

Whatever your goal, your environment should be seen as a tool that can be used to help inspire you and thrust you towards your goal. It should not hinder you or hold you back in any way. We are constantly bombarded by sensory information that seemingly has an insatiable appetite for our attention. As well as things such as phones, tablets and televisions we often get distracted by other people. This could be our parents, children, partners, the Amazon delivery driver, the list goes on indefinitely. Being 'distracted-free' for a defined period of time is something that I'm willing to bet that most people almost never experience. Creating an environment where you have zero distractions and a space that inspires and allows you to do deep work is crucial to your success.

Where is your environment? For example, the gym, my studio, my desk.

List up to 5 things in your current environment you believe are hindering your efforts toward your goal: For example, I bring my phone into my studio whilst practising the piano, or the gym is way too busy after work to get on the equipment I want so I rarely complete a full workout.

1.
2.
3.
4.
5.

List up to 5 things that if you had in your environment you believe would help you achieve your goal: For example, a quiet and distraction-free space to practice the piano or two uninterrupted hours per day.

The Mental Toughness Workbook

1.

2.

3.

4.

5.

An easy and obvious solution to this would be to leave your phone in another room or at the very minimum turn your phone to 'do not disturb' for a period of time whilst you practice and have regular short breaks for 5 minutes. If you cannot put your phone down then taking it with you to where you're supposed to be learning, training, and being creative is just robbing your amount of productive uninterrupted time.

TIP

Sometimes the most obvious and simple answers are the right ones. If stuck between a simple solution or a complicated solution, the simple solution is almost always going to be the right one. This is because simpler solutions frequently have fewer moving parts.

The next question is not meant to pass judgment or blame but rather to help you understand how and why you don't get that 'distraction-free' time you need to accomplish your goal. Be honest, not judgmental.

List the top 5 people you believe take up the most of your time. These can include family, work, social or other commitments: For example, my two children or my friend Rick.

1.

2.

3.

4.

5.

And lastly, it can be easy to overlook how you are spending your time. Do you know how much free time you actually have? If your desired goal is outside of your current working hours for your job, you are already losing a considerable amount of time for the day. But don't fret, it will just require more creativity and perhaps more patience. Below, work out how you spend your average workday and an average day off. Include your sleeping routine, travel time, eating times etc.

00:00

_____

01:00

_____

02:00

_____

03:00

_____

04:00

_____

05:00

_____

06:00

_____

07:00

_____

08:00

_____

09:00

_____

10:00

_____

11:00

_____

12:00

_____

13:00

_____

14:00

_____

15:00

_____

16:00

_____

17:00

_____

18:00

_____

19:00

_____

20:00

_____

21:00

_____

22:00

_____

23:00

_____

The Mental Toughness Workbook

Now do the same for your average day off.

00:00

_____

01:00

_____

02:00

_____

03:00

_____

04:00

_____

05:00

_____

06:00

_____

07:00

_____

08:00

_____

09:00

_____

10:00

_____

11:00

_____

12:00

_____

13:00

_____

14:00

_____

15:00

_____

16:00

_____

17:00

_____

18:00

_____

19:00

_____

20:00

_____

21:00

_____

22:00

_____

23:00

_____

Now calculate the times in the table below.

Activity	Time spent per day Weekday (x5)	Total Weekday	Time spent per day Weekend (x2)	Total Weekend	Total Sum
Sleeping					
Working					
Commuting					
Eating					
Cleaning/Maintenance					
Workout					
Watch TV					
Socialising					
Other					

TIP

A good way to see how much time you are wasting a day is by looking at your phone's daily usage. Latest studies reveal that about a third of an average person's waking time per day is spent on their phone and this does not include work-related activities. That's roughly 5 hours a day!

What could you be doing with that extra time?

Understanding who and where you spend most of your time will help guide you when it comes to creating your winning environment and your daily routines. If you spend all evening after work on your Xbox and tell people you wish you could speak Spanish or play the guitar but don't have time, you won't be getting much sympathy from me.

The Mental Toughness Workbook

Perhaps your environment is the gym, perhaps it's a studio or it may even just be your laptop and headphones but all of these environments have moments where they can hinder your success or moments when they can offer you pure distraction-free opportunities. By going through the above and understanding who and where you spend your time it helps to paint a picture in your mind about where you are currently at and what changes need to be made. You don't have to go all out right away. Minor changes to daily routines and environments are what create success over the long run.

Below are some examples of problems related to your environment and potential, simple solutions.

Problem

You're an aspiring bodybuilder but your current gym workouts suffer because you go to the gym at 6 pm after work when it's super busy and not only do you have to wait longer to get on the equipment but, a few of your old pals go and you get caught up chatting about your day instead of focusing on working out.

Solution

A minor change to this could be to go to the gym before work or go later on in the evening. Both may offer some uncomfortable truths such as "I hate mornings enough already without getting up an hour earlier" or "I enjoy relaxing in the evenings" but you have to ask yourself how badly do I want this (my bodybuilding goal) if I can't stomach sacrificing either of the two above statements?

Problem

I just don't have the time to learn Spanish as my time is completely taken up by parenting in the evenings after work.

Solution

I will get up half an hour earlier on weekdays to practice Spanish. That's already 2.5 hours a week or nearly 5 and half days a year that you could be learning Spanish! That's **ONE** minor change. You will be tired, you will feel it the first few days and maybe even weeks but you **WILL** get used to it. You can then increase the time as you become more accustomed to waking up early.

TIP

An easy, and often overlooked solution to gaining 'extra' time to do the things we want, is to simply look at cutting the things in your life that are already not working for you. Most people aren't blessed with an abundance of spare time in their day so taking things out of your routine such as stopping off for a coffee on the way to work every day can open up opportunities for something else to take its place if that's what you want.

Why Self-Discipline is Different from Mental Toughness

"The ability to continue moving when you are feeling scared, fearful or lazy is the sign of true mental strength."
– Matthew Donnelly

Mental toughness is a mindset and an attitude that you acquire. It is shaped through the adoption of values like resilience, determination, courage, overcoming adversity, and assuming full responsibility for every aspect of your life.

Self-discipline is a tool that you use for acquiring greater mental toughness by habitually doing what is necessary to get closer to your goal(s).

You don't stop working when you are feeling tired and exhausted. You stop only when you are finished. You don't show grit and determination on some days and let it fizzle out on other days. You abide by your core values every single day despite the circumstances. This is what self-discipline is.

Starting strong and staying strong are very much two different types of discipline.

Consistency

"Success is the sum of small efforts, repeated day in and day out."
– Robert Collier

The difference between champions and everyone else is that champions don't do what's needed only when they feel like it. They get out of bed even when their body is aching and it is freezing cold outside. They show up every single time they are supposed to.

Being consistent is so important when it comes to accomplishing your goals and objectives. After all, it's only when we stop trying and give up can we truly say that we have failed.

Being consistent is a grind. It's your hustle. You have to get into your head that at times it's going to make you uncomfortable, bored, or even disillusioned. The power of consistency though should not be underestimated. Routinely staying consistent can offer exponential changes over a longer time frame. The trouble is they can be hard to spot at the time and can make you feel demotivated. This is why having something to measure your activities such as a consistency log can help.

Below is a 7-day consistency tracker. Even tracking the small goals you accomplished throughout the week can really help keep you inspired going into the next week. It can be something to look back and reflect on, offering you an opportunity to see where you have had good days/weeks or perhaps bad ones. This is important and can help you to spot trends.

7-day consistency tracker:

Things I've done/completed today. List up to 5 things. For example, I went to the gym. I finished editing my book. I did my tax return. Don't worry if you don't have 5 items and don't worry if the task seems trivial like making your bed, they all count.If you prefer to focus on one thing at a time, that's cool.

Monday:

1.

2.

3.

4.

5.

Tuesday:

1.

2.

3.

4.

5.

Wednesday:

1.

2.

3.

4.

5.

Thursday:

1.

2.

The Mental Toughness Workbook

3.

4.

5.

Friday:

1.

2.

3.

4.

5.

Saturday:

1.

2.

3.

4.

5.

Sunday:

1.

2.

3.

4.

5.

Looking back at what we've done daily we can reflect and begin to analyze our days and how productive we are. Again, this isn't to pass judgment but rather, to serve as a platform for us to gather data and look for potential opportunities to develop better habits or routines. It can also be an opportunity for us to build confidence and acknowledge that we are on the right path.

I suggest buying a journal/notepad or creating a word document where you can continue to log past the 7 days above. You will thank yourself later for doing so.

Get comfortable being uncomfortable (Adversity)

"Everything you want lies just outside your comfort zone."
– Robert G. Allen

Mediocrity loves comfort! Because their drive to be at ease outweighs their ambition to thrive, the majority of people never reach their potential. They don't want to take risks or deal with challenges. In whatever circumstance, they choose the one that is the easiest.

By engaging in conventional activities, one can never become great. Your everyday routine holds the key to success. This is how champions are made.

Below is an adversity log for you to use. Write in this when you've done something you didn't particularly enjoy doing or better, was going to put off. Nothing is too mundane or unworthy. An example could be:

What did I do that I didn't want to do? *Go for a run.*

Why didn't I want to do it? *Because it was raining, heavy!*

How do I feel now that I've completed it? *Happy! I've worked out for the day when I could have easily skipped it.*

Adversity log

What did I do that I didn't want to do?	Why didn't I want to do it?	How do I feel now that I've completed it?
1.		
2.		
3.		
4.		
5.		
6.		
7.		
8.		
9.		
10.		

Having the ability to look back at challenges or things you didn't want to do or thought you could not do, can give you the visual cues needed to believe that you are capable of more than you give yourself credit for. You can implement this into your journal, diary or word document.

Being self-disciplined means acting with consistency. Consistency is always better than any spur of fleeting motivation. Consistency is what builds results.

Be consistent in your discipline and disciplined in your consistency.

You are wasting your time if you aren't making continuous, firm progress toward your goals every single day. Self-discipline and mental toughness go hand in hand. They are interrelated. To succeed in anything in life, you require both of them in equal proportion.

Failure

"Anyone who has never made a mistake has never tried anything new."
– Albert Einstein

You might ask yourself, how do I know I'm becoming mentally stronger?

Failure!

It's how you react to a situation or experience and how you strive and adapt. Every bad moment in life leaves you with two options:

1. Live in self-pity and become defeated.

2. Accept the lesson, learn and improve. Come back with a better attitude.

Failure does not have to be fatal. Failure is a great measuring stick for assessing how mentally tough you are. 6 months ago you dreaded the idea of failure. It paralysed you into inaction. Now you run head first into the same thing that terrified you because if you fail, there's a lesson to be learned and if you don't…Well, then you win!

You know you can use the grit you have developed to achieve even better things in life every time you think back to anything challenging that you overcame by pure tenacity and drive.

It's easy to fail. It's harder to confront the fact you failed in something and have that deep level of self-reflection and analysis that's required to overcome your challenge. It's even harder when you fail time and time again. Failure should not be feared if you are genuinely learning though.

After all, you miss 100% of the shots you do not take.

Your new start-up was a washout. You didn't get picked for the college football team. You just received a call from the interview you attended and you did not get the dream job. These all suck but if you want to become a truly mentally tough, self-disciplined and driven person you will need to learn to stand your ground and face failure in the face and see it for what it is. An opportunity to learn and grow.

Below is a failure log. Not one that's supposed to intimidate you or make you feel sad but one where as a result of your failure you learned something new or managed to turn it around and get the win you wanted. Don't worry if you can't fill this in yet but as you continue to grow and believe in yourself and your abilities come back to this and fill it in.

1. What you failed at.

_____

_____

What you learned.

_____

_____

2. What you failed at.

_____

_____

The Mental Toughness Workbook

What you learned.

_____

_____

3. What you failed at.

_____

_____

What you learned.

_____

_____

4. What you failed at.

_____

_____

What you learned.

_____

_____

5. What you failed at.

_____

_____

_____

What you learned.

_____

_____

Circle of Control

"You have power over your mind, not outside events. Realize this, and you will find strength."
– Marcus Aurelius

We've spoken a lot about things you can implement yourself in order to get you closer to your desired goal, mental state of mind or desired result. Now it's time to understand the things in our lives we cannot control.

We know we can't control the weather, other people's opinions of us, or even the results of our efforts.

This does not stop them from having an enormous impact on our mindset, mood and actions. It hurts more when somebody says something negative about us than it makes us happy when somebody says something nice. We remember the things we failed at with dread and embarrassment but shrug off and downplay the things we got right, including big achievements as the bare minimum of our expectations. Not something to be overly excited about.

I agree, that we shouldn't revere forever in our personal achievements or from the opinions of people who praise us but we must equally not spend too much of our time waisting mental energy on trying to control events, words, and actions that are not within our control.

Understanding this can be hard at first, but it is 100% liberating when you start to implement it. It's very easy to say that you should not get upset or pay too much attention to the fact you didn't get selected for your college basketball team this semester but we all know, as humans it can deeply affect us.

The truth is that you can put in all the effort in the world but that still does not mean you will get what you want from your efforts. I'd be a football player if the world worked like that.

We always, always, always though have the ability to control what's within our circle of control. We can put the training in. We can invest in learning and honing our skills. We can seek the advice of a mentor.

We can never control what happens to the ball once it's left our hand though.

We do get to control how we choose to respond to external events, opinions or actions from people. We get to decide that by missing that title winning shot we have the option to go again. To learn again and improve.

When you are prepared to go the extra mile for however long it takes, you are a true champion already. You have a vision for how you want everything to go, but you are not emotionally invested in the details of how or when it will actually happen. You have complete faith and self-assurance in the fact that you already own everything you desire. Your vision *will* eventually come to pass and become a part of physical reality.

Let's find out what's in your circle of control.

What's in your circle of control? For example, my response to a setback or the effort i put into running my new start-up company.

-
-
-
-
-
-
-
-
-

What's not in your circle of control? For example, the opinions of others about my goals.

-
-
-
-
-
-
-
-
-

Realize what's in your circle of control and everything else becomes noise.

Integrity

"If you're tired of starting over, stop giving up."
– Shia Labeouf

You must accept complete responsibility for your life if you want to succeed. It doesn't end there; you must spend each and every day of your life with unwavering integrity and be completely responsible for your own actions. While accountability and integrity cannot be shared, responsibility may often be in many different spheres of life. Being accountable is accepting responsibility for not only who you are, what you are going through, and what you are doing, but also for your actions.

Integrity is who you are when no one is looking. Keep your standards high at all times because you are constantly being watched by the person inside of you, not because other people could see you.

Accountability is the strength to accept responsibility for all of your actions—good, terrible, and ugly. When you make a mistake, it's the capacity to accept that you made a mistake. It involves looking carefully at yourself and accepting your own weaknesses.

Below is an integrity log. Fill this in when you feel you did something with integrity when perhaps you could have taken the easier route. For example:

Activity

- Only doing 9 of the 10-mile run I had planned.

Consequence avoided

- Anger and frustration for taking the easy route.

Mentorship

"If you cannot see where you are going, ask someone who has been there before."
– J Loren Norris

We are in the most fantastic period of human history. You can watch, read or listen to some of the greatest minds in history with only a click of a button. Whatever your objective or goal, you need a mentor if you want to achieve it with great success. I'm not advocating that you get one-on-one coaching in order to benefit from having a mentor. It may or may not be practical for you, depending on the nature of your aspirations and your financial condition right now, but mentors can save you a lot of time, effort and potentially money.

We live in a period where at the click of a button we can search for anything and everything in the world. If I want to learn about the pharaohs I can hop online, search for it and thousands of articles, blogs, newspapers and videos will appear in a microsecond. However, we've all fallen victim to the paradox of choice, and this is where a mentor can come in handy.

Having a good mentor enables you to save time, frustration and perhaps even jump the cue. Do not mistake having a good mentor for taking your foot of the gas though. They are where they are because they've grafted, probably had a mentor themselves and learned from hundreds, maybe even thousands of tiny errors along the way. A champion athlete might tell you where your training could improve, what the best equipment is to use and how your diet needs improving but that doesn't mean you'll be standing on the podium anytime soon. **YOU** have to put the effort in!

Honing your own skill set, routines and mental conditioning is what makes you unique but asking for advice from somebody who has been there and done that before you is a sure-fire way to improve your all-around game, save time and evolve.

Below, write down 5 people who already do what you do and whom you would like to be mentored. For example, if you want to be a pro boxer you could say Muhammad Ali.

1.

2.

3.

4.

5.

Now, sticking with the boxer theme you have 5 different boxers or coaches that you can learn from. They'll most likely all have books written by them and others, done countless TV interviews I'm willing to bet will be on Youtube as well as thousands of hours of fight and training clips.

You'll be able to find out what gym they trained at, for how long, who coached them, what they ate, how many sit-ups and press-ups they did a day, what ounce gloves they trained in as well as almost anything else you might desire to know.

You don't have to know somebody on a personal level to benefit from their expertise. If you do however that's even better.

Community

"Alone, we can do so little; together, we can do so much."
– Helen Keller

Another great tool to add to your tool bag is becoming part of a community that shares your objectives, goals or personal interests. Just like having a mentor can provide you with a wealth of expertise, communities offer you the opportunity to observe, interact and meet people whom you can learn from or offer to help yourself.

TIP

Offering help to people who are on the same journey as you is a great way to gauge the knowledge you think you have about a subject and can be brilliant at helping you spot blind spots in your knowledge.

By engaging in these communities you are fed an endless amount of data about your subject from people who are living it as well as opportunities for learning and collaboration.

These communities are everywhere nowadays in the digital world. They're on social media platforms such as Facebook (Meta), Youtube, Reddit etc. They're in blogs you can subscribe to. They're even in book clubs. Communities are everywhere and whatever your interests are, there is guaranteed to be a whole community available, ready and waiting to accept you.

Thinking of your desired goal/objective, write down 5 places you could expect to find a community. For example, if your goal is to run an ultra-marathon then there are already hundreds of Facebook (Meta) groups awaiting your invitation or magazine subscriptions that you can join. Physically, in the real world, there are groups of people that will regularly meet up and train together. The list is endless. Get inspired!

1.

2.

3.

4.

5.

7-day reflection and analysis

Already, in this workbook, we've set the foundations for a stronger mindset. But before we continue it's a good time to look back at our new routines, new logs etc to see how we're getting on. Reflection and self-analysis should not be overlooked. By looking back at what we've done and how we've done it, it offers us the chance to see what's working and what's not. It gives us the chance to spot trends and enables us to implement changes where needed. You can do this on a weekly basis, a monthly basis or even a daily basis if you wanted to.

What has worked over the past 7 days?

_____

_____

_____

In what areas do I think I can improve?

_____

_____

_____

What has not worked in the last 7 days?

_____

_____

_____

Why did it not work?

_____

_____

_____

How can I improve this?

The Mental Toughness Workbook

_____

_____

_____

It can be hard to spot the small wins but by using this workbook I hope it can become a little sanctuary for you to see just how on track you are.

Before we continue I would urge you to ensure that all the exercises and questions are completed. Once these are completed fill in the Mental Toughness assessment again below. This might seem fruitless after a week or two of using this workbook but if you're somebody who has never had a routine but now consistently does, understands what is in their circle of control and has done things they usually would not then I hope you will be amazed at how much of an improvement in your score there will be.

Scores from 1-10. 1 meaning not at all and 10 meaning absolutely.	1-10
1. I believe that I can achieve anything I set my mind to.	
2. I believe I have full control over all aspects of my life.	
3. I have the confidence in my abilities to achieve my desired goals and ambitions.	
4. I have the confidence in my abilities to try new things I'm interested in.	
5. I have a solid record of completing my goals and objectives.	
6. My environment is free from distractions and enables me to perform at my best.	
7. I generally look after my health, including my physical fitness, my mental wellbeing and my emotions.	
8. I actively look for ways to improve all aspects of my life.	
9. My goals align with my core values.	
10. The goals and dreams I am actively pursuing are mine and mine alone.	
TOTAL SCORE	

0-30 Just Getting Started

60-75 Amateur Mental Toughness

75-90 Pro Mental Toughness

90-100 Elite Mental Toughness

"Trust yourself. You know more than you think you do."
– Dr Benjamin Spock

In the first part of this workbook, you analyzed your baseline Mental Toughness. You figured out your *why* your values and principles and you wrote down your desired goal or purpose of this workbook.

In Part 2 you created a roadmap for your journey towards concrete Mental Toughness. You created a winning environment. You analyzed how and where your time was spent and with whom. You learned about the power of consistency and implemented this into your routine. You created an uncomfortable log to show yourself that you *can* and *do* finish things that you don't like doing but know will benefit you in the long run. You set up a failure log to remind yourself of the times you tried, and failed, but learnt something about yourself that will make you even stronger in the future. You developed an understanding of your circle of control and learned how to use it to your advantage. You learnt the value of integrity and identified that the only person you're ever cheating with is yourself. You seeked out mentorship from people whom you admire and aspire to be like. You embraced the communities you wish to be a part of. And finally, you looked back on all of this with non-judgemental, self-analysis and reflection in the knowledge that you are well on your way to becoming the person you know you can be.

In part 3 we go get what's ours!

3

PART 3 CONTINUATION TRAINING

"We are what we repeatedly do. Excellence, therefore, is not an act but a habit."
– Aristotle

If you want to achieve an elite level of mental toughness then you do what's needed, not when it's easy or convenient, but when it needs to be done.

That was the last line of my summary of what I think Mental Toughness is at the start of this book. I hope by now you can see that Mental Toughness isn't something that's just given to you at the end of this workbook. It's accumulated from the thousands of tiny choices **YOU** make day in and day out. It's a sum of all the wins and all the losses you make and how you choose to deal with them.

The high motivation inside of you for the first couple of weeks when trying something new is always going to wane, eventually. This is why I have not mentioned motivation in this book and nor do I believe motivation can be something to be relied upon, or trusted. Motivation is the little devil on your shoulder that wants you to do something only when they want to and will have nothing to do with you when they are not interested.

Elite Mental Toughness, the kind that extreme mountaineers have or elite fighting forces, is not born from motivation but from doing what's necessary every single moment of their lives. They don't complete their goals, pat themselves on the back and wait for accolades.

They push themselves into new territory they didn't know was possible and for no other reason than.

They live and breathe the lifestyle they wish to have.

Part 3 is your continuation training. It's the accumulation and the continuation that's needed from you to grow and progress. You'll find nothing new here. Just everything you learnt in this book so far over and over again. With each passing week and month, you are afforded the opportunity to see your growth. To see how you've learnt and how you've developed.

Mental Toughness isn't a destination, it's a journey!

What are you waiting for?

Week 2

"Twenty years from now, you will be more disappointed by the things you didn't do than by the ones you did do. So throw off the bowlines. Sail away from the safe harbour. Catch the trade winds in your sail. Explore. Dream. Discover."
– Mark Twain

7-day consistency tracker:

List up to 5 things you complete each day.

Monday:

1.

2.

3.

4.

5.

Tuesday:

1.

2.

3.

4.

5.

Wednesday:

1.

2.

3.

4.

5.

Thursday:

1.

2.

3.

4.

5.

Friday:

1.

2.

3.

4.

5.

Saturday:

1.

2.

3.

4.

5.

Sunday:

1.

2.

3.

4.

5.

Adversity log

Fill in the table if you overcome adversity this week.

What did I do that I didn't want to do?	Why didn't I want to do it?	How do I feel now that I've completed it?
1.		
2.		
3.		
4.		
5.		
6.		
7.		
8.		
9.		
10.		

Failure Log

Below is the Failure Log for the week. Fill this in when you tried, but failed to meet your expectations and consequently the lessons you've learnt from it.

TIP

Don't worry if you do not know the immediate lesson. It may take days, weeks, months or even years before you truly understand the lesson learned. Just come back to this when you do and fill in accordingly.

1. What you failed at.

_____

_____

What you learned.

_____

_____

2. What you failed at.

_____

_____

What you learned.

_____

_____

3. What you failed at.

_____

_____

What you learned.

_____

_____

4. What you failed at.

_____

_____

What you learned.

_____

_____

5. What you failed at.

_____

_____

What you learned.

_____

_____

Circle of Control

What is within your circle of control this week and what is not?

-
-
-
-
-
-
-

-
-

What's not in your circle of control?

-
-
-
-
-
-
-
-
-

Integrity Log

Below is an integrity log for the week. Fill this in when you feel you did something with integrity when perhaps you could have taken the easier route.

Activity	Consequence avoided
1.	
2.	
3.	
4.	
5.	
6.	
7.	
8.	
9.	
10.	

Mentorship

Write the top 5 things you've learnt this week from your new tutors. For example, I listened to a podcast about the training regime Muhammad Ali used to do daily.

1.

2.

3.

4.

5.

Community

List the top 5 things you learnt from or did for others in your community this week.

1.

2.

3.

4.

5.

7-day reflection and analysis

Complete a 7-day reflection and self-analysis for the week. The aim is to look at what we've done well and look to improve in areas we might have fallen short of this week. If changes are needed then jot them down and implement them the next week.

TIP

Some things can take time to see results so it's important to bear in mind that a week might not be enough to dismiss something entirely. You wouldn't rip up and change your weight loss training routine after a week because you haven't lost any weight. It's important to understand what may take time to show the desired results.

What has worked over the past 7 days?

_____

_____

_____

In what areas do I think I can improve?

_____

_____

_____

What has not worked in the last 7 days?

_____

_____

_____

Why did it not work?

_____

_____

_____

How can I improve this?

_____

_____

_____

The Mental Toughness Workbook

Week 3

"Change what you can, manage what you can't."
– Raymond McCauley

7-day consistency tracker:

List up to 5 things you complete each day.

Monday:

1.

2.

3.

4.

5.

Tuesday:

1.

2.

3.

4.

5.

Wednesday:

1.

2.

3.

4.

5.

Thursday:

1.

2.

3.

4.

5.

Friday:

1.

2.

3.

4.

5.

Saturday:

1.

2.

3.

4.

5.

Sunday:

1.

2.

3.

4.

5.

Adversity log

Fill in the table if you overcome adversity this week.

What did I do that I didn't want to do?	Why didn't I want to do it?	How do I feel now that I've completed it?
1.		
2.		
3.		
4.		
5.		
6.		
7.		
8.		
9.		
10.		

Failure Log

Below is the Failure Log for the week. Fill this in when you tried, but failed to meet your expectations and consequently the lessons you've learnt from it.

1. What you failed at.

_____

_____

What you learned.

_____

_____

   2. What you failed at.

_____

_____

What you learned.

_____

_____

   3. What you failed at.

_____

_____

What you learned.

_____

_____

4. What you failed at.

_____

_____

What you learned.

_____

_____

5. What you failed at.

_____

_____

What you learned.

_____

_____

Circle of Control

What is within your circle of control this week and what is not?

-
-
-
-
-
-
-
-
-

What's not in your circle of control?

-
-
-
-
-
-
-
-

Integrity Log

Below is an integrity log for the week. Fill this in when you feel you did something with integrity when perhaps you could have taken the easier route.

Activity	Consequence avoided
1.	
2.	
3.	
4.	
5.	
6.	
7.	
8.	
9.	
10.	

Mentorship

Write the top 5 things you've learnt this week from your new tutors. For example, I listened to a podcast about the training regime Muhammad Ali used to do daily.

1.

2.

3.

4.

5.

Community

List the top 5 things you learnt from or did for others in your community this week.

1.

2.

3.

4.

5.

7-day reflection and analysis

Complete a 7-day reflection and self-analysis for the week. The aim is to look at what we've done well and look to improve in areas we might have fallen short of this week. If changes are needed then jot them down and implement them the next week.

What has worked over the past 7 days?

_____

_____

_____

In what areas do I think I can improve?

_____

_____

_____

What has not worked in the last 7 days?

_____

_____

_____

Why did it not work?

_____

_____

_____

How can I improve this?

_____

_____

_____

Week 4

"You can have anything you want if you are willing to give up the belief that you can't have it."
– Dr Robert Anthony

7-day consistency tracker:

List up to 5 things you complete each day.

Monday:

1.

2.

3.

4.

5.

Tuesday:

1.

2.

3.

4.

5.

Wednesday:

1.

2.

3.

4.

5.

Thursday:

1.

2.

3.

4.

5.

Friday:

1.

2.

3.

4.

5.

Saturday:

1.

2.

3.

4.

5.

The Mental Toughness Workbook

Sunday:

1.

2.

3.

4.

5.

Adversity log

Fill in the table if you overcome adversity this week.

What did I do that I didn't want to do?	Why didn't I want to do it?	How do I feel now that I've completed it?
1.		
2.		
3.		
4.		
5.		
6.		
7.		
8.		
9.		
10.		

Failure Log

Below is the Failure Log for the week. Fill this in when you tried, but failed to meet your expectations and consequently the lessons you've learnt from it.

1. What you failed at.

_____

_____

What you learned.

_____

_____

2. What you failed at.

_____

_____

What you learned.

_____

_____

   3. What you failed at.

_____

_____

What you learned.

_____

_____

   4. What you failed at.

_____

_____

What you learned.

_____

_____

5. What you failed at.

_____

_____

What you learned.

_____

_____

Circle of Control

What is within your circle of control this week and what is not?

-
-
-
-
-
-
-

-
-

What's not in your circle of control?

-
-
-
-
-
-
-
-
-

Integrity Log

Below is an integrity log for the week. Fill this in when you feel you did something with integrity when perhaps you could have taken the easier route.

Activity	Consequence avoided
1.	
2.	
3.	
4.	
5.	
6.	
7.	
8.	
9.	
10.	

Mentorship

Write the top 5 things you've learnt this week from your new tutors. For example, I listened to a podcast about the training regime Muhammad Ali used to do daily.

    1.

    2.

    3.

    4.

    5.

Community

List the top 5 things you learnt from or did for others in your community this week.

1.

2.

3.

4.

5.

7-day reflection and analysis

Complete a 7-day reflection and self-analysis for the week. The aim is to look at what we've done well and look to improve in areas we might have fallen short of this week. If changes are needed then jot them down and implement them the next week.

What has worked over the past 7 days?

_____

_____

_____

In what areas do I think I can improve?

_____

_____

_____

What has not worked in the last 7 days?

_____

_____

_____

Why did it not work?

_____

_____

_____

How can I improve this?

_____

_____

_____

Week 5

"No one can make you feel inferior without your consent."
– Eleanor Roosevelt

7-day consistency tracker:

List up to 5 things you complete each day.

Monday:

1.

2.

3.

4.

5.

Tuesday:

1.

2.

3.

4.

5.

Wednesday:

1.

2.

3.

4.

5.

Thursday:

1.

2.

3.

4.

5.

Friday:

1.

2.

3.

4.

5.

Saturday:

1.

2.

3.

4.

5.

Sunday:

1.

2.

3.

4.

5.

Adversity log

Fill in the table if you overcome adversity this week.

What did I do that I didn't want to do?	Why didn't I want to do it?	How do I feel now that I've completed it?
1.		
2.		
3.		
4.		
5.		
6.		
7.		
8.		
9.		
10.		

Failure Log

Below is the Failure Log for the week. Fill this in when you tried, but failed to meet your expectations and consequently the lessons you've learnt from it.

1. What you failed at.

_____

_____

What you learned.

_____

_____

2. What you failed at.

_____

_____

What you learned.

_____

_____

3. What you failed at.

_____

_____

What you learned.

_____

_____

4. What you failed at.

_____

_____

What you learned.

_____

_____

5. What you failed at.

_____

_____

What you learned.

_____

_____

Circle of Control

What is within your circle of control this week and what is not?

-
-
-
-
-
-
-
-
-

What's not in your circle of control?

-
-
-
-
-
-
-
-

Integrity Log

Below is an integrity log for the week. Fill this in when you feel you did something with integrity when perhaps you could have taken the easier route.

Activity	Consequence avoided
1.	
2.	
3.	
4.	
5.	
6.	
7.	
8.	
9.	
10.	

Mentorship

Write the top 5 things you've learnt this week from your new tutors. For example, I listened to a podcast about the training regime Muhammad Ali used to do daily.

1.

2.

3.

4.

5.

Community

List the top 5 things you learnt from or did for others in your community this week.

1.

2.

3.

4.

5.

7-day reflection and analysis

Complete a 7-day reflection and self-analysis for the week. The aim is to look at what we've done well and look to improve in areas we might have fallen short of this week. If changes are needed then jot them down and implement them the next week.

What has worked over the past 7 days?

_____

_____

_____

In what areas do I think I can improve?

_____

_____

_____

What has not worked in the last 7 days?

_____

_____

_____

Why did it not work?

_____

_____

_____

How can I improve this?

_____

_____

_____

Week 6

"Pain unlocks a secret doorway in the mind, one that leads to both peak performance, and beautiful silence."
– David Goggins

7-day consistency tracker:

List up to 5 things you complete each day.

Monday:

1.

2.

3.

4.

5.

Tuesday:

1.

2.

3.

4.

5.

Wednesday:

1.

2.

3.

4.

5.

Thursday:

1.

2.

3.

4.

5.

Friday:

1.

2.

3.

4.

5.

Saturday:

1.

2.

3.

4.

5.

Sunday:

1.

2.

3.

4.

5.

Adversity log

Fill in the table if you overcome adversity this week.

What did I do that I didn't want to do?	Why didn't I want to do it?	How do I feel now that I've completed it?
1.		
2.		
3.		
4.		
5.		
6.		
7.		
8.		
9.		
10.		

Failure Log

Below is the Failure Log for the week. Fill this in when you tried, but failed to meet your expectations and consequently the lessons you've learnt from it.

1. What you failed at.

_____

_____

What you learned.

_____

_____

2. What you failed at.

_____

_____

What you learned.

_____

_____

3. What you failed at.

_____

_____

What you learned.

_____

_____

4. What you failed at.

_____

_____

What you learned.

_____

_____

5. What you failed at.

_____

_____

What you learned.

_____

_____

Circle of Control

What is within your circle of control this week and what is not?

-
-
-
-
-
-
-

-
-

What's not in your circle of control?

-
-
-
-
-
-
-
-
-

Integrity Log

Below is an integrity log for the week. Fill this in when you feel you did something with integrity when perhaps you could have taken the easier route.

Activity	Consequence avoided
1.	
2.	
3.	
4.	
5.	
6.	
7.	
8.	
9.	
10.	

Mentorship

Write the top 5 things you've learnt this week from your new tutors. For example, I listened to a podcast about the training regime Muhammad Ali used to do daily.

1.

2.

3.

4.

5.

Community

List the top 5 things you learnt from or did for others in your community this week.

1.

2.

3.

4.

5.

7-day reflection and analysis

Complete a 7-day reflection and self-analysis for the week. The aim is to look at what we've done well and look to improve in areas we might have fallen short of this week. If changes are needed then jot them down and implement them the next week.

What has worked over the past 7 days?

_____

_____

_____

In what areas do I think I can improve?

_____

_____

_____

What has not worked in the last 7 days?

_____

_____

_____

Why did it not work?

_____

_____

_____

How can I improve this?

_____

_____

_____

Now that our 6 weeks are over, fill in the mental toughness self-assessment questionnaire again. Over time you will notice that the results are getting better. This is just the beginning.

Scores from 1-10. 1 meaning not at all and 10 meaning absolutely.	1-10
1. I believe that I can achieve anything I set my mind to.	
2. I believe I have full control over all aspects of my life.	
3. I have the confidence in my abilities to achieve my desired goals and ambitions.	
4. I have the confidence in my abilities to try new things I'm interested in.	
5. I have a solid record of completing my goals and objectives.	
6. My environment is free from distractions and enables me to perform at my best.	
7. I generally look after my health, including my physical fitness, my mental wellbeing and my emotions.	
8. I actively look for ways to improve all aspects of my life.	
9. My goals align with my core values.	
10. The goals and dreams I am actively pursuing are mine and mine alone.	
TOTAL SCORE	

0-30 Just Getting Started

30-60 Well On My Way

60-75 Amateur Mental Toughness

90-100 Elite Mental Toughness

75-90 Pro Mental Toughness

Conclusion:

Well done for making it to week 6 and I hope you found this workbook useful and inspiring. I hope that within the pages you've discovered insights about yourself, whether that be in your mental, physical or emotional state that you did not know before. I hope this workbook can offer you comfort and act as a reference to guide you on your journey to a stronger, healthier mindset.

Life isn't always easy and it's seldom a straight line between point A and point B. Where you are now and where you want to be. Just remember that we all have ups and we all have downs. We all have good days and bad days. We sometimes have bad weeks, months, and years. Just know, however, that the power to change is within you and all wins, no matter how small build up, accumulate and compound over time. The same goes both ways, however.

So find something you are passionate about and become a lifelong student. Enjoy the ride and take knowledge in the fact that you are learning from both wins and losses. Failure is not something to be avoided or something that should bring shame and embarrassment to you but something that can offer you an opportunity to learn and grow.

With self-discipline and mental toughness comes an impenetrable fortress in your mind. A ring of fire that only you have the option and power to let things into. There's a clear distinction between what's achievable *now* and what *can* be achieved in the future.

NOTES

The Mental Toughness Workbook

The Mental Toughness Workbook

Printed in Great Britain
by Amazon